Beautiful America's

Oregon Coast

Beautiful America's

Oregon Coast

By Linda Stirling

Photography by Larry Geddis

Beautiful America Publishing Company

Front cover: Breaker at Shore Acres State Park

Opposite title page: The needles at Cannon Beach

Published by
Beautiful America Publishing Company
P.O. Box 244
Woodburn, OR 97071

Library of Congress Catalog Number 91-6784

ISBN 0-89802-721-7
ISBN 0-89802-720-9 (paperback)

Printed in Korea

DEDICATION

With heartfelt thanks to the friends who add joy to my life: Michael and Sylvia Eagan, Pat Bresnahan, Gail McIntyre, Cherie Veys, Robert Foote, Jr., Bill Greene, Gillian Francis, Dannelle and John MacCorkindale, Victoria Crumpacker, Jason Baron, Matt and Tana Phemeister, David and Kathy Weil and Rich Cohen. Special thanks to my women's group, the sisters of my heart, and to my crew of dancing buddies – without whom life wouldn't be such fun. Much love to all my family, especially my children, Keith, Kevin, Kari, Audra and Jordan, and to my grandchildren, Dillon and Kole. Thanks to my Mom, for being my friend. Not to be forgotten on my list of life's best people are Ted and Beverly Paul – they don't come any better than you two. And last, but first in my heart, Joseph Grandy III.

Linda Stirling

Ecola State Park and Cannon Beach

Seagulls in flight at Haystack Rock

The annual Sand Castle Contest at Cannon Beach

Contents

Introduction

While the United States has many beautiful areas, the Oregon Coast displays a majesty that captures your spirit. There is such *power* in the coast's beauty, the crashing rhythm of its waves, the immensity of towering Douglas fir or Sitka spruce that line its terrain, and its craggy up-thrust shores – power in the seeming perpetuity of coastal splendor. With that everlasting quality comes a peaceful essence, too, a feeling bestowed when you have the chance to sit and watch waves lapping against a rising sun, or fog slinking through the trees as it is chased by a breeze.

The delights of the coast are bountiful, the choices of activities difficult only because of their appealing variety. Of course, many pleasurable hours could be spent just exploring rock formations that jut daringly out to challenge the ocean, or following a trail of hoof prints that lead off in dark gold sand.

Whole vacations could be spent pursuing one small portion of coastal activities. One might select whale watching, a kite flying festival, exploring lighthouses or a myriad of other activities. Such choices might take you up and down the coast, or you might prefer to choose one of the wonderful towns as a destination, since all of the towns on the coast are delightfully explorable, being small enough to walk around, yet versatile enough to keep anyone's interest over a period of many visits.

If a meander around town is not your cup of tea, the Oregon Coast Highway (U.S. 101) provides a bike ride to remember. Or the boat ramps and access points along the coast provide numerous boating and fishing opportunities. There are first-rate golf courses, historical sites and museums aplenty and, with some planning, you could spend days or weeks trekking some of the lovely hiking or

A rare sight, snowfall on the "Three Graces" near Garibaldi

Opposite page: Sunrise at Ecola State Park

walking trails that ribbon the area.

Should you prefer to travel by car, the Oregon Coast Highway is the most-traveled and perhaps most-loved route, but there are some splendid alternative drives with their accompanying "alternative" scenery on less traveled backroads. As the appreciation of the coast increases, it becomes more and more necessary to make reservations if you plan on spending the night. At the very least, obtain your lodging early in the day while there are still spots to be reserved.

Whenever you travel along the Oregon Coast, you'll find yourself mesmerized by the cadence of waves against the shore, mesmerized by the brilliant melange of colors and sights. And if you're fortunate enough to call the coast your home, you'll know you're there when, at the end of the day, you crest the hill and the trees are black-fringed silhouettes against a sapphire sky that is still tinged with the pinks of the sun's good-bye. Surely the Oregon Coast is heaven on earth.

Walk on the Wild Side
The Road Less Traveled

Just north of the Cape Perpetua Visitor Center lies one of the "alternative scenery" drives, this one winding towards Yachats. Along this route there are interpretive signs explaining forces of nature and policies of forest management. Most of this trip focuses on the delights of the forest rather than the ocean, as there is only one ocean viewpoint. But be aware, you may have to share this road with logging trucks on the weekdays.

Another great drive is the Carpenterville Road from Pistol River to Brookings. This route climbs a ridge and provides a panoramic ocean view within the Boardman State Park.

Rough roads keep many travelers off the route from Powers to Agness – and they keep them away too from the stunning view of the Rogue River and the Rogue Wilderness. If perfect pavements aren't a necessity for you, this could become a favorite jaunt. To travel back to the coast from this area, the road along the Elk River back to Port Orford will add further pleasure to your drive.

If heading out on foot has been your intention all along, there's an absolute wealth of walking trails on the Oregon Coast. With thousands of miles of trails to choose from, there are a few that stand out because they offer both beauty and the advantage of being less frequently traveled.

Two separate routes along the 375-mile Oregon Coast Trail can take you up Neahkahnie Mountain, which towers 1,631 feet above sea level. Known to the Tillamook Indians as "the home of the fire spirit," Neahkahnie rests between Arch Cape and Manzanita. The mountain lies within the boundaries of Oswald West State Park, and routes to its top will lead you through deep forest, lush meadow and scenic open areas near the peak's rocky summit.

Sunset at Twin Rocks

Three Arches National Wildlife Refuge at Oceanside

One section of the Oregon Coast Trail is the Tillamook Head National Recreational Trail, which lies primarily within the Ecola State Park boundaries. Although the trail is located near the popular tourist towns of Cannon Beach and Seaside, the trail is not used excessively. Your choices for usage might include a two-mile walk from Indian Point to a stunning viewpoint on Tillamook Head, an overnight backpacking trip to a hiker's camp near Tillamook Head, or a six-mile trek to Seaside.

Near the lovely town of Lincoln City you will find another trail quite worthy of your time. Harts Cove Trail lies within the Cascade Head Scenic Research Area in the Hebo Ranger District of the Siuslaw National Forest. Creeks trickle across your path, sea birds cruise the sky and, once you reach the bright grassy meadow that overlooks the Pacific, you may see sea lions or even whales. This trail is a charmer, combining the fresh, invigorating scent of spruce trees and sea air.

Another area to explore on foot is a nine-square mile preserve called the Drift Creek Wilderness. Near the town of Waldport, and lying within the Siuslaw National Forest, this is an area lush with stands of old-growth rain forest – among the largest remaining in the United States. Its steep, timbered ridges roll down to remote streams, canyons, and small, open meadows that are accessible only by trail.

Also within the Siuslaw National Forest is the Gwynn Creek Trail near Cape Perpetua. This route is an easy one to take. It starts near the Cape Perpetua Visitor Center and follows the Oregon Coast Trail for a while, retracing the early wagon road that once linked Florence and Waldport. After about a mile, it links with the Gwynn Creek Trail, climbing to the Gwynn Creek Canyon, taking you through large stands of old growth Douglas fir and Sitka spruce. You can retrace your steps or loop back to the Visitor Center along a 6.5 mile trail.

If you love the bubbling spray of waterfalls, Kentucky Falls (east of Florence) are actually a series of three very distinct falls lying on Kentucky Creek and the North Fork of the Smith River. They can be approached by taking a well-maintained

1890 Cape Meares Lighthouse

footpath that passes through stands of old-growth forest. Maps for the area can be obtained by stopping off at the Mapleton Ranger Station, approximately 15 miles east of Florence on Highway 126.

A solitary beach that offers twisted, polished driftwood and other delights, such as an occasional sand dollar or a glass float from Japan, is the Winchester Bay oceanfront. This seven-mile stretch is closed to vehicles and provides the perfect opportunity for wave watching, sand digging and quiet contemplation.

Other beaches you'll want to walk are those south of Cape Arago. Accessible through the Seven Devils State Wayside off Highway 101, Agate Beach, Sacchi Beach, and Merchants Beach are noted for their agates and small pieces of petrified wood.

Don't take off your hiking boots until you've had a chance to get to one of the most stunning ocean views available. Travel to the short trail that begins just south of the Merchants Beach Visitor Center on Highway 101. This trail leads to the Cape Perpetua viewpoint and it is here that, on a clear day, you can see the coast as it stretches north to Cape Foulweather and south to Cape Blanco. At an elevation of 803 feet, it is the highest viewpoint so close to the ocean.

When you have had a chance to scout the many trails and it's time to settle down in a campground or stop to rest your feet at a park, there are plenty of choices. All of the Oregon Coast parks and campgrounds are, like the rest of Oregon, kept refreshingly clean. Any park you run across will provide a peaceful respite, but some parks stand out.

If it's solitude you seek, there are six hiker/boater campsites on the shore of Siltcoos Lake. These camps are primitive, with only fire rings, tables, and privy-type toilets, so you have to be prepared to pack in your gear, but the setting here is so stunning the trek is worth it. To hike in, take the Siltcoos Lake Trailhead, eight miles south of Florence, and follow the two-mile trail through the forest to the shore of Siltcoos Lake. Boaters' camps nestle along the west shore of Siltcoos.

North of Gold Beach lies the 100-acre Honey Bear Campground. This lovely campground has plenty of space for either recreational vehicles or tent camping.

Although lovely any time, the Cape Sebastian State Park south of Gold Beach is alive with wildflowers in late April and May. Pacific Paintbrush, snow-queen, rein orchid, Douglas' iris, black crowberry, and goldfields (found only in this coastal region) are abloom. Camera buffs and wildflower enthusiasts will have a heyday with the banquet of color.

This is just a taste of the wide variety of camps and parks available.

Some of the Oregon Coast's offerings are to be had only by chance. A trip to see the white tundra swans that winter in the shallow marsh lakes of the Oregon Dunes Recreational Area from November through January might result in sighting only a bird or two. On the other hand, you might come upon hundreds of the stately birds stretching their wings and calling to each other across the water. So, too, is it by chance that you may spot migrating gray whales, or see some of the many other marine mammals in the coastal waters.

Most Oregon campsites now require reservations, so do plan ahead.

Fort Clatsop National Memorial

Astoria Column

The Lightship Columbia, part of the Columbia River Maritime Museum at Astoria

Around Astoria
Absorb Some History

Sure bets for sightseeing are the towns that merge their charm with that of the land's delights.

On the northwestern tip of the Oregon Coast lies Astoria, named after John Jacob Astor. It sports the distinction of being the oldest American settlement west of the Rockies.

In May of 1792, Captain Robert Gray discovered the Columbia River where it reaches the ocean and he sailed inland as far as Tongue Point. In December 1805, Captains Meriwether Lewis and William Clark completed their expedition from St. Louis and built Fort Clatsop, where they wintered over in preparation for the long trip back. Then, in 1811, John Jacob Astor's men established a fur trading post on the bank of the Columbia River and named it Astoria.

Today, Astoria is being rediscovered by tourists who want to take a step back in time. The city itself is composed of Victorian cottages layered on a hill above the wharf and city center, and many of these restored Victorian-style homes are open for tours. The best way to find out what's available for viewing is by making the Captain George Flavel Mansion your first stop. Here, you can see the most lovely of homes, plus pick up a map for further touring.

Captain George Flavel was a pioneering Columbia River Bar Pilot, and the area's first millionaire. In 1885, he built the beautiful Queen Anne-style home on grounds that encompass a city block. Since 1950, the home has been operated as a museum by the Clatsop County Historical Society.

This elegant historical focal point features high-ceilinged rooms with elegant woodwork, décor, and furnishings that are still impressive. The six fireplace mantels alone are worth seeing. Each is carved from a different hardwood and accented by a special tile imported from a city in Europe and Asia.

Astoria is also home to the Columbia River Maritime Museum on Astoria's waterfront. Recognized as one of the finest collections of its kind on the West Coast, the museum preserves the maritime heritage of the Columbia River basin and the north coast area. The museum's Great Hall houses a collection of fishing and rescue craft and several exhibits. And then there are seven thematic galleries to interpret the region's maritime history: Fur Trade & Exploration; Navigation and Marine Safety; Fishing, Canneries & Whaling; On The River; Sailing Vessels; Steam & Motor Vessels; and Naval History. In all, there is over 24,000 square feet of exhibit space which houses an enormous collection of artifacts, models, paintings and other art. On weekends you can usually catch a display of rope-making or net-mending. Children can peer through real submarine periscopes or take the helm of a schooner. Outside the museum is the lightship *Columbia*, the last U.S. Coast Guard lightship to serve on the Pacific Coast.

If your historical tastebuds have been whetted by a visit to the Maritime Museum, you can satisfy them further by stopping at the Heritage Museum. The building itself has a rich history, having served as a City Hall, Clatsop County offices, a library, a USO club for pre and post World War II servicemen, and the first home of the Columbia River Maritime Museum. Here, you can expect to see exhibits of Native American artifacts, nautical history, early settlement exhibits, logging exhibits, commercial fishing history and artifacts concerning the twenty-two ethnic groups that have lived in Clatsop County. There is also a first-rate art exhibit and a rich collection of photography that deals with Astoria and Clatsop County from the late 1800's until the late 1930's. A few blocks away there is even a Fire Fighters Museum – it was home to a popular brewery from 1896 until 1915, when it was shut down because of Prohibition.

The best known symbol of Astoria would perhaps be the Astoria Column. Descendants of fur trader John Jacob Astor and the Northern Pacific Railway are responsible for the construction of the column, which was dedicated in 1926. At

The Lewis and Clark statue at the Seaside turnaround

Opposite page: Breaker at Cape Kiwanda

the time, the Northern Pacific Railway was building monuments in cities all along its rail system. Patterned after the Trajan Column erected in Rome by Emperor Trajan in 114 A.D., the monument rises 125 feet to survey the surrounding countryside. The energetic may climb the steps for a breathtaking view of the lower Columbia River and the Pacific Ocean. On a clear day you may even see the altered cone of Mount St. Helens, which erupted in May 1980. The outside of the column exhibits a mural created by Italian artist Atillio Pusterla. This wonderful mural spirals up the outside of the tower, depicting the history of the area from the time its primeval forests were discovered by Captain Robert Gray. At the base of the monument a large relief map, cast in bronze, points out landmarks visible on the surrounding countryside. While it does not rank in size with many monuments and memorials in different countries, the fact remains that it is the only large piece of memorial architecture of reinforced concrete finished with a pictorial frieze in sgraffito work.

Another attention-getter is the Astoria Bridge. Long popular in television commercials and general photography, the bridge is a stunning piece of architecture. At 4.1 miles across, it has the distinction of being the longest continuous truss span bridge in the world. It is designed to withstand some of the toughest attacks of nature. Wind gusts of 50 miles per hour from the fierce Pacific storms that occasionally batter the coast still leave the bridge with a safety factor. The concrete piers are built with an eye towards the river flood speed of nine miles per hour, which can be the case during floods when the raging water sometimes sweeps along whole trees.

To really soak up a feeling of the past, you can't leave the Astoria area until you've traveled the six miles down Highway 101 to the Fort Clatsop National Memorial. This is the site of the stockade that Captains Meriwether Lewis and William Clark built to weather over during the winter of 1805. During the three months of winter they put up game, made moccasins and buckskins to replace their worn-out clothing, and prepared in other ways for their long homeward trek.

The fort deteriorated over the years, but in 1955 a replica was built on the site. Today, over 200,000 have visited to see the fort's "Living History" program where national park rangers make candles, smoke meat, make clothing, build canoes from a single spruce log, and shoot with the old muzzle-loading muskets in the same way the expedition members did.

Nearby, Fort Stevens has more than 600 campsites, including sites for recreational vehicles. A network of trails for hiking or biking connect the campgrounds with the beach. One of the attractions is the ghostly, rusting hulk of the Peter Iredale, an English four-masted sailing ship that was driven aground by a winter storm in 1906.

Fort Stevens was built during the Civil War. Closed as a military post in 1947, its history has been preserved in a museum as well as in the remaining battery and gun emplacements. The fort was the only mainland installation fired on by a Japanese submarine during World War II.

The Astoria area is also attractive to fishermen. Historically this has been a great fishing area because it is here that the mouth of the Columbia River joins the sea. The fishing is some of the finest and most consistent in the world. Halibut, ling cod, rockfish, sturgeon, and, in midsummer, shark and tuna are here in abundance . . . and then there's always the silver lightning bolt of the Northwest, the salmon.

Commemorating the Indians whose lifestyle was so heavily dependent on the fishing, a 26-foot cedar log statue stands at Smith Point in Astoria. This tribute to the Clatsop and Chinook Indians was created by Peter "Wolf" Toth. The statue's name, Ikala Nawan, means "Man Who Fishes." The Indian sculpture wears a fishing hat commonly worn by the Clatsop and Chinook Indians. The hat, says Toth, was generally made of the inner bark of the cedar tree, buffalo grass, or other materials. The cedar log used for Ikala Nawan is over 500 years old.

The view south from Cascade Head

Sunset at Haystack Rock, Pacific City

Take in More Towns
Seaside to Cannon Beach

Seaside, the Pacific Northwest's largest beach resort community, is a charming stop for any traveler. A two-mile promenade of shops, restaurants and arcades offers a glorious feast for both those who love to buy and those who love to window shop. Even in the largest big-city malls, you couldn't find the variety (not to mention the unusual finds) of merchandise to be discovered on the strip of this bubbling town. "Handmade" and "quality craftsmanship" are labels for a good portion of the merchandise; so if you want unique sweaters, pottery, dolls, and other items that will continue to be treasures over the years, this is the place to shop. In Seaside, as in all the towns along the Oregon Coast, nature melds with man; so the turnaround at the end of the promenade doubles as access to the town's expansive beach.

There are a couple of other promenades in town – both charming in very different ways. The first is a two-mile stretch lined with charming old beach homes, the second is a promenade of trained seals at the Seaside Aquarium.

If you schedule your visit just right, you may take in the Yuletide Festival, a February jazz festival, or an August volleyball tournament that is played on the beach. Any time of year you can see the marker commemorating the end of the Lewis and Clark Trail, or you can visit a replica of the salt cairn that was used by the Lewis and Clark expedition to boil seawater in the winter of 1805-1806. Young or old, the eyes of the travelers in your group will light up when you stop by the antique carrousel with its twenty wooden horses, all nestled under a giant skylight.

After you've had a proper tour of town you might want to take off along one of the numerous hiking trails in the local area. There are too many to easily choose from, some being designated trails that begin at state parks and make loops back into the forest or meander along the headlands, others merely skirting along through the woods or winding near a river or creek.

Of the established trails, four are noted favorites. Saddle Mountain Trail is a one-day hike that culminates at the highest point in the Coast Range (3,238 feet). You should allow two hours going up, and one-and-a-half hours coming back. If you prefer, you can travel to Saddle Mountain State Park by taking Highway 26 to the sign just past milepost 15. The seven-mile drive from Highway 26 to the base of Saddle Mountain proves a great view of the coast on clear days.

Tillamook Head Trail is a six-mile hike in and back. You can start either at Indian Beach in Ecola State Park, or at the entry south of Seaside. The trail traverses a cape jutting out into the sea between Cannon Beach and Seaside. Local historians believe this was probably the route Lewis and Clark took when they came to Ecola Creek in 1806.

Another lovely hike can be had by taking the Neah-Kah-Nie Mountain trail. This is a shorter excursion that offers as its particular charm some ever-widening views of 30-mile stretches of the coast.

A final recommendation is the Cape Falcon Trail. Origination point is Oswald West State Park. While the hike is only two miles each way, you'll want to allow plenty of time to view the wonderful coastal rain forests.

Seaside and Cannon Beach are close sisters in beauty as well as in a plethora of activities. One difference native Oregonians think of when they think of Cannon Beach is Haystack Rock, for this spectacular free-standing monolith is a visual trademark of the area. Jutting up 235 feet from the water near the beach, the rock is a natural investigative site for studying inter-tidal habitats and nesting birds. Members of the Haystack Rock Awareness Program instruct visitors on the wonders of this marine resource.

Taking its name from the monolith, the Haystack Program in the Arts and Sciences, put on by Portland State University, turns Cannon Beach into a temporary

Boiler Bay State Park

artists' colony each summer. Well-respected instructors, many of whom are nationally known, converge to meet with the small groups who gather to further their knowledge of writing, calligraphy, watercolor technique, bluegrass instrument instruction and more. It's an inspiring setting that sends the participants away greatly enriched.

While some items of beauty such as Haystack Rock are anchored firmly upon the earth, others have to be recaptured because of the minds that bring them back into creation each year. Such is the case of Sand Castle Day. Originally designed for children, the adults wouldn't let go of the fun, so for over a quarter of a century both children and adults have gotten out their buckets and trowels for a day of play in the sand. Of course, a bit of one-upmanship was bound to happen, for who doesn't want to build a better sand castle? The result has been some of the finest sand sculpturing in the world. Each year new splendors are constructed. In the past there have been constructions of Cinderella and her carriage, the Titanic, and Humpty Dumpty – the expressions as varied as the crews that come to happily construct them. And then there's always that kid on the outer border of all the adult activity: his overall straps have been freed, his straggly blond hair fights with the wind, he wipes his nose with a sandy hand and digs in again with a cup and a spoon to pile up the mound that is a masterpiece only in his eyes. Hours later, everyone's treasures will be smoothed out by the ocean and memories become more substantial than sand.

Other memories can be collected by visiting some of the parks around Cannon Beach.

Ecola State Park marks the site where Lewis and Clark and Sacajawea ended their journey. Clark noted the site as a "butifull sand shore." His journey across Tillamook Head was prompted by his interest in purchasing a supply of whale meat from Indians who had a small village on Ecola Creek. On his visit he recorded that there was a whale's skeleton on the beach that was 105 feet long. He purchased 300 pounds of meat from the Indians there, along with a few gallons of

"The World's Smallest Harbor" – *Depoe Bay*

A charter fishing boat enters Depoe Bay

20-pound tuna, iced and ready for market

oil, and wrote, "thank Providence for directing the Whale to us; and think Him much more kind to us than He was to Jonah, having sent this Monster to be swallowed by us in sted of swallowing of us as Jonah's did."

It was this site, too, where one of the early settlers, a sailor named John Gerritse, hauled a cannon out of the ocean near Arch Cape. The cannon was determined to have come from the U.S. Survey Schooner Shark, which wrecked on Clatsop Spit just inside the mouth of the Columbia River on September 10, 1846. It is said that two other cannons were discovered at the same time and that when Gerritse went back to recover them they had again been buried by the shifting sands. If that is true, there may be a time when the tides again wash away the sand and reveal their whereabouts.

In 1953 two cannons, constructed to resemble the originals, were placed at each entrance to the community of Cannon Beach.

Other parks around the area are just as history-steeped and fun to visit. Whale Park, Les Shirley Park, and Arcadia Park are all pleasant stops.

South of Cannon Beach three striking headlands – Arch Cape, Cape Falcon, and Neahkahnie Mountain are showcased by Oswald West State Park. A short hike down the beach brings you to Smuggler's Cove, reputedly a pirate's haven in years gone by. You may want to set camp in the area so you can search for the 18th century treasure chest that's said to be buried somewhere on Neahkahnie Mountain.

Say Cheese
Tillamook's Dairyland

You'll say "cheese" and much more when you visit the Tillamook area. It's famous for its cheeses (and ice cream!) but it also serves luscious helpings of pastoral scenery and rich history.

In Indian language, Tillamook means "land of many waters" – an apt description. Tillamook's lush grasses, nurtured by as much as 75 inches of rain a year, sustain the herds that compose Oregon's dairy industry.

Much of the county's annual milk production of 25 million gallons is made into natural cheddar cheese at the Tillamook Cheese Factory just north of town. The factory attracts more than 800,000 visitors each year who stop in to buy souvenirs and have an ice-cream cone.

Don't miss another great cheese stop: the Blue Heron Cheese Company, which is housed in a blue and white barn surrounded by pastures. Here, you can sample distinctive Brie and other cheeses, dips, and Oregon wines while you browse the gift shop. Outside, there's an informal petting zoo that's free to the public.

In addition to its agricultural importance, Tillamook is a major recreational center. Seven streams, the gentle rains and the mild climate combine to make this a pleasant place to live or to play. Charter boats for crabbing and deep sea fishing are available. Jetty, river, and surf fishing, clamming and beachcombing are popular activities at the beach areas nine miles west of town. Hiking, hang gliding, scuba diving, windsurfing and canoeing are also among the area's offerings.

Taking you back through the past, the County Pioneer Museum holds one of the state's best displays of pioneer memorabilia, including pioneer quilts, clothing and guns, native baskets and arrowheads. There's even a replica of the house

The home of Tillamook Cheese

Kite flying at Newport Beach

made out of a tree that the area's first white settler, Joe Champion, lived in.

Bird watchers come to Tillamook to look for great blue herons in the tidal flats of the bay and to see thirty waterfowl species. Fishermen cast their lines in the Kilchis, Wilson, Trask, Tillamook and Miami rivers, and bicyclists follow the county's byways.

You might want to leave Tillamook by route of the Three Capes Scenic Drive. This 40-mile loop serves as the gateway to some of the most diverse coastal scenery to be found in Oregon, and offers a look, too, at the salt marshes and commercial oyster-shucking operations along Tillamook Bay. At the top of Cape Meares, a short hike leads to an abandoned lighthouse and the accompanying views of offshore islands that teem with sea birds and sea lions.

If you're hungry when you get through sightseeing, there are a number of fresh seafood and other specialty restaurants, many offering cozy settings with surfside views. Drive a short distance to Netarts Bay and you can feast upon grilled crab and blackberry pie.

A cluster of other little towns are a short drive from Tillamook. Garibaldi is a deep sea port for charter and commercial fishing; Nehalem, which in Indian means "place of peace," has a great little winery and park; Manzanita is a resort community; Wheeler hosts the annual Nehalem Bay canoe races; Rockaway Beach features wide sandy beaches, fishing and swimming lakes, shopping and recreation; and Twin Rocks and Oceanside offer places to stay within easy distance of agate hunting.

Go Fly a Kite
Near Lincoln City

There's plenty more to do in Lincoln City and the surrounding towns than fly a kite, but you'll certainly want to revive your kite flying skills when you crane your neck at the aerial displays of kites in vivid colors, startling sizes, and fantastic styles.

Each May and September the town hosts a kite flying festival that's earned it the title of Kite Capital of the World, but any time of year the kites are in the air.

Lincoln City is an angler's paradise year round, too. Ocean charter fishing trips can be arranged out of Depoe Bay, or you can fish the Siletz River for Chinook salmon, steelhead and trout. The Siletz Bay offers perch, crab and flounder. Devil's Lake, which is open year round, has trout, perch, catfish, crappie and largemouth bass.

Lincoln City has a new billing as a shopper's Mecca. The Quality Factory Village houses discount stores for over 45 popular brand-name businesses.

The funky little town of Depoe Bay is billed as having the smallest harbor in the world. Highway 101 is the main street here, and nothing but a sea wall separates the town from the often angry Pacific. A rough winter storm can sometimes hurl the breakers right over the highway.

A sizeable fleet of fishing boats make their home in this tiny harbor, and whale-watching cruises leave from here as well. You can also watch for whales from the cliffs above the ocean or the small restaurants that line the highway make good vantage points. One, the Whale Cove Inn, even provides binoculars!

Look for the "D" River – the world's shortest river. The "D" empties into the ocean from Devil's Lake, a popular area for water-skiing, sailboating, windsurfing and camping.

Rocky Creek State Park at its lava rock shoreline

Cape Perpetua from Strawberry Hill State Park

43

Gleneden Beach, just south of Siletz Bay, is home to the five-star resort, Salishan. Here, you'll be treated to excellent service, gourmet dining, an acclaimed wine list, oceanside golf, and what else? – shopping.

Also near Depoe Bay is a popular spot called Boiler Bay Wayside. The power of the ocean is evident both here and at the Spouting Horn, where seawater shoots skyward as it is forced through crevices in the basalt rock cliffs.

Tourists' Delight
In the Newport Area

Long a favorite vacation spot, Newport and the nearby countryside have continued to blossom with activities that delight every age group. Whether you're on the fast track of life or seek to slow things down a little, there's plenty to draw from around here. The delightful ocean views, exciting winter storms and generally moderate temperatures add to the attraction.

If you enjoy outdoor activities, the area teems with all types of possibilities. A high percentage of people try their hand at crabbing, clamming, boating or fishing – and here you have a chance to try offshore, onshore or river fishing. The county is drained by five major rivers that flow into the Pacific. These rivers terminate in estuaries at the Pacific – the largest of which is Yaquina Bay in Newport. The bonus is that the ideal environment is created for marine life – oysters, clams and crab in the bays, and a large variety of fish including trout, steelhead and sturgeon in the rivers. The ocean yields salmon, shrimp, halibut and an assortment of rockfish. If fishing is too tame for you, there's always the option here of taking up sailing, surfing or hang gliding!

"Must do" activities in this area include stops at some of the community's notable learning centers and visitor attractions.

Listed as one of the top 500 attractions in the country, the Marine Science Center on Yaquina Bay is the coastal research, teaching and marine facility for Oregon State University. The Science Center sponsors whale watching programs during the winter and has a good aquarium and museum.

If sea creatures attract you, you must not miss the Undersea Gardens. Here, a wonderful display of marine animals and plants is housed. Scuba diving shows are held regularly.

The sandstone cliffs of Otter Crest, Devil's Punch Bowl State Park

Morning at Seal Rock State Park

While you're touring the town, check out the Wax Works and Ripley's Believe It Or Not. Animated wax figures will take your breath away at the Wax Works and you'll hold it again when you see the displays of bizarre and unusual mysteries of nature and technology housed at Ripley's.

A sampling of the area's history can be had at the Lincoln County Historical Society Museums. One is a log cabin museum holding Indian artifacts, pioneer farm equipment, logging and maritime exhibits; the other is the Burrows House, which contains period furniture, clothing and pioneer exhibits. For more modern exhibits, you won't want to miss the Yaquina Art Center, and for plays, musicals, and other shows, the new 300-plus seat theatre at the Newport Performing Arts Center provides a wide variety of artistic entertainment.

If you're of a literary bent, you could experience a stay that you'll never forget at the Sylvia Beach Hotel. This charming hotel was built between 1910 and 1913, and was renamed and put on the register of historic landmarks a few years ago. Its name is a tribute to Sylvia Beach, the 1920's and 30's owner of the Shakespeare and Co. Bookstore in Paris. Beach was one of the century's greatest patrons of literature. As lovely as the hotel itself is, the real attraction is the way the rooms are laid out. Each of the twenty guest rooms have been furnished and named after different authors such as Agatha Christie, Mark Twain, Dr. Seuss, Edgar Allen Poe and Willa Cather.

For a visit back in time, tour the Yaquina Bay Lighthouse. The lighthouse was constructed in 1891 as a harbor entrance light for Yaquina Bay and is the only surviving example in Oregon of a lighthouse with a combined keeper's dwelling and light tower. The lighthouse also is the oldest existing building in Newport. Its light went out in 1874 and was never reactivated. Restoration of the lighthouse was completed by the Oregon State Parks and Recreation Division in 1975. Authentically refurbished with furnishings appropriate to the historic period, it is operated by the parks division as a house museum with interpretive history exhibits. It is open to the public during the summer months.

Sunset at Yaquina Head Lighthouse

Fishing fleet at Newport Bay

The 1871 Yaquina Bay Lighthouse at Newport

The Oregon Coast Aquarium, rehabilitation home of Keiko

Visitors observe outdoor tidal pools at Oregon Coast Aquarium

The 1938 Yachats Covered Bridge in Lincoln County

Kentucky Falls on Oregon's central coast

Oregon Dunes National Recreation Area

Heceta Head light at Devil's Elbow State Park

Opposite page: Heceta Head Lighthouse

Sunset at Whale's Head Beach

Breaker at Shore Acres State Park

Shore Acres, just as pretty during the holidays

Opposite page: Spring at Shore Acres Botanical Garden

Cape Arago Lighthouse

Beautiful Bandon Beach

Early morning solitude at Bandon

A Bandon Beach sunset

The small town of Seal Rock is noted for its craft shops with their wares of jewelry, ceramics, and large chainsaw-carved wood sculptures. The Seal Rock Wayside State Park provides an opportunity for clamming, surf fishing, hiking and picnicking.

Nestled along the mouth of the Alsea River, Waldport is popular among salt- and freshwater fishermen. The coastline on both sides of Alsea Bay varies from smooth sandy beaches to rugged rocky formations. Hiking, agate hunting, clamming, and crabbing are popular pursuits in many of the state parks in the area.

The small village of Yachats gathers its share of the anglers in Oregon. They arrive for the smelt season, which occurs every year between April and October. This is one of the few areas in the world where hundreds of these sardine-like fish come to shore to spawn. Besides smelt fishing, the Yachats River is a popular spot for salmon and steelhead fishing. Other popular pastimes include beachcombing, rockhounding, bird watching and painting. A perfect spot for the painting easel is Cape Perpetua, just south of town. Cape Perpetua is the highest point on the Oregon coast, and it offers a dramatic ocean view from its 800-foot headland.

Nestle up to Nature
Near Florence

What creature looks cuddlier than a fat old sea lion? A few miles north of Florence the Sea Lion Caves are home to hundreds of Stellar sea lions. As fascinating as the animals themselves is the cave that soars to the height of a twelve-story building and stretches the length of a football field. Formation of the cave began about 25 million years ago and today it is a richly multi-hued geologic wonder that is among the largest and most beautiful caves in the world. The tour includes scenic pathways that take you to an elevator that carries you 208 feet down into one of the largest sea caves in the world.

If you stop by the caves during the spring and early summer, you'll find the lions outside on the rookery where they do their breeding and birthing. Here, too, you may see some of the largest of the bulls, some weighing up to a ton . . . maybe "cuddly" isn't the best word.

The city of Florence is, in itself, a delightful place to spend some time. Known as the City of Rhododendrons, the dramatic scenery of the area is enough to recommend it as a stopover. There are breathtaking views of rugged coastline, miles of magnificent beaches and spectacular mountains of sand at the Oregon Dunes National Recreation Area. Florence's picturesque harbor, where fishing boats lie against a backdrop of the restored buildings of Florence's Old Town, is a delightful place. The surrounding countryside, where colorful wild rhododendrons spring from a landscape of lush, verdant forests and where babbling brooks come down to meet the barnacle-covered rocks of the sea, has a charm that piques the senses.

Over 2,000 campsites are available, many near the ocean, while others are tucked away in the woods near creeks and freshwater lakes. Outdoor action is the

Humbug Mountain and Three Sisters Rocks at Gold Beach

Samuel Boardman State Park

main theme, for you can water ski, scuba dive, spear fish, jet ski, sailboat, sailboard, canoe, river raft, or jump in one of the great old-fashioned swimming holes. If that doesn't drain your energy, there's always the sand dunes and a buggy ride, or a romantic horseback ride along the beach.

A different and fun way to spend a morning is by clamming or crabbing. Along the muddy flats of the Siuslaw River, you'll find some of the best clamming anywhere. You can purchase or rent some crab rings, too, and by dinner time you'll have a seafood feast. What better way to prepare it than on a campfire near the beach? When morning comes you'll want to walk near the waves to see if the Japanese Current has washed ashore any glass fishing floats, Philippine mahogany logs or even some Eskimo or Indian artifacts.

Take your camera with you on your morning walk and throughout the day. The tidepools offer endless hours of fascination with starfish, anemones, rock crabs and other interesting small sea life. Birds abound – sandpipers and snowy plovers scamper along the edge of the surf in search of tasty morsels, and dark cormorants keep busy building their nests of grasses and seaweed on broad flat ledges before heading out to dive to depths as great as 180 feet for fish.

If you find time to walk through the forests, you may run across raccoons, deer, brown bear, or Roosevelt elk. You may even be so fortunate as to see a bald eagle as it dives over the water to snatch up a dinner of trout.

A charming piece of area history is maintained in Heceta House, not only by its inclusion of the National Register, but with its recognition as a "ghost house."

In 1975 the *Siuslaw News* read, "Lady of the Lighthouse Baffles Workmen." A family named Tammens had moved into the Innkeeper's House near the Heceta Head Lighthouse. Shortly after moving into the dwelling known as Heceta House, they reported "ghostly manifestations." A series of unexplained events convinced the couple that no natural phenomena could be responsible for the commotion.

It is said that at a card party one night, the Tammens and their guests heard what they described as a high-pitched scream. At other times, cupboard doors definitely shut at night were open the next morning, and rat poison left in the attic was exchanged for a single silk stocking.

Others, too, noted strange occurrences. The evidence was substantiated by workmen who had been commissioned to do painting and repair projects at the house. Tools began to disappear and mysteriously reappear in the same spot. Padlocks opened without explanation.

A workman named Jim Anderson claimed he was cleaning a window in the attic one day when he noticed strange reflections in the glass. He turned around and caught a glimpse of a gray-haired, elderly woman dressed in a 1890's style gown. She peered at Anderson out of a wrinkled face. Anderson left and refused to return to the site for some days – and he never would reenter the attic. But he hadn't heard the last from the ghost.

While working on the exterior of the house, he accidentally broke an attic window. He repaired it from the outside, leaving the broken glass inside on the attic floor. That night, the Tammens woke to what they said sounded like glass being swept from the attic floor – though they had no knowledge of the window being broken earlier. The next morning they went up and the glass had indeed been swept into a neat pile.

A peaceful coexistence has been formed by the occupants of Heceta House, though the identity of the ghost is uncertain. Some claim her name is Rue, and a long-abandoned grave nearby forms the center of the speculation of the gray lady's identity. It is said the grave is that of a baby girl, presumably the daughter of an early innkeeper. Some say the ghost is the baby's mother, who has come back in search of her child, while others say that Rue is the child.

Mack Arch and Crook Rock on southern coast

Cape Sebastian

By the Bay
Coos Bay, That is

The town of Coos Bay revolves its business around the busy port that has become one of the busiest export stations for forest products in the world. Coos Bay and her neighboring town of North Bend offer visitors a glimpse of busy port city activities and so much more.

Charleston, a fishing village at the mouth of Coos Bay that has been described as "Mediterranean," is a good spot to track back to so you can catch the Cape Arago Highway. From there you can travel to Sunset Bay State Park. The park encompasses a semi-circular lagoon that's protected by overlapping fingers of rock. It is one of the safest swimming places on the coast.

One of the most delightful attractions in the area is the Shore Acres State Park. It features formal English gardens, a Japanese pond, and flowers that have been brought in from around the world. Here, the combination of the gardens, the rugged shoreline, the sandstone bluffs, and a covered observatory combine to create a photographer's paradise.

A natural wonder is the Oregon Dunes National Recreation Area. Forty-one miles of dunes extend from North Bend to Florence. The area encompasses 32,000 acres of dunes, marshes and forestland. In addition to black-tailed deer and unique plants and other wildlife, over 270 bird species call this home. The dunes were formed within the last 10 to 15 thousand years as ocean currents distributed the sand along the shore. The area is a welcome open space for those who like to hike, surf fish, crab, clam and roam the beaches.

Among the many other parks to visit, some particularly pleasant stops are Small Boat Basin, in Charleston; Sunset Bay State Park; Tenmile Lakes; and the South Slough National Estuarine Reserve. There are also numerous small delightful historical museums ranging from a logging museum to a newspaper museum. And don't forget the lighthouse tours!

Traveling south on Highway 101 you'll reach the coastal village of Bandon. Along this route you will see what many believe to be the most beautiful beach views in Oregon. Natural sea sculptures such as Elephant Rock, Table Rock, and Face Rock call out for use of a camera.

Climate So Fair
Near Brookings and Port Orford

Lying within a coastal "banana belt," the Brookings Harbor and Port Orford areas have much to offer in addition to the pleasant weather.

The collection of craft stores, gift shops, galleries and charming restaurants that proliferate elsewhere along the Oregon Coast can be found here too. Also in keeping with many other Oregon shops, a great number of the pieces available are sold only in this area or are made in limited quantities. You'll find antique jewelry, vintage toys, handmade porcelain dolls, quilts rich with color, hand-wrought silver jewelry and so much more.

The towns are surrounded by deep forests, there are turquoise rivers and freshwater lakes, and you can still find times when the beaches will be entirely your own.

Over 300 species of birds make the area their home at various times of the year, and wildflower enthusiasts will be spellbound – the climate allows for an almost year-round blooming season.

Near Brookings, the Azalea State Park, a botanical park that is often a favored bird-watching spot, blooms with azaleas from April through June. Loeb State Park

300 to 800-year-old protected redwoods near Brookings

Opposite page: Cranberry harvest near Bandon

is one spot where you can see the myrtlewood trees, and the Oregon Redwood Trail takes you along many lovely streams where canopies of huge redwood trees loom overhead and rhododendrons mark your passage.

For a dusting of the past, visit Whaleshead Beach State Park where the cove-rock formation has a blow hole which resembles a whale's head. This is also a goldmining site and some old abandoned mining equipment is still lying about – so, too, is the memory of the rumrunners who landed illegal booze here during Prohibition.

The Pistol River area, fun for many other reasons, also offers a bit of history. It was in February and March of 1856, during the Rogue Indian Wars, that men hastily constructed a fort of driftwood and held off the Indians until relief troops from California arrived.

One bit of the Brookings/Port Orford history has a very touching ending. In 1942, an incendiary bomb was dropped by a plane assembled aboard a Japanese submarine that lay offshore. The pilot flew over Mount Emily and dropped several bombs, but only one caused damage, and that damage came in the form of a forest fire. (This was the only spot in the continental United States to ever be bombed by a foreign power.) The pilot had made that flight with a good luck charm tucked under his seat: the cherished Samurai sword that had been passed on in this family for more than 400 years. The man's name was Nobuo Fujita. He returned to the area in 1962 with a gift of atonement – the same Samurai sword he had carried with him twenty years before.

Nobuo Fujita's return in 1962 was received with the same spirit of welcoming that visitors to the area receive today; and in this lies the most vivid wealth of the coast – this, the spirit of generosity, joy and goodwill that the people of this area exude. And it is also through them and their covenant with the land and sea that the beauty of the area remains for all of us to enjoy.

About the Author

Oregon Coast is one of three books Linda Stirling has written for Beautiful America. She has been a published writer for over twenty years and has several hundred articles in print, in addition to her books. She's worn the hat of publisher, both with a company of her own and as the managing editor for another company. One of her greatest delights has been working with other writers. She wrote for and was the managing editor of the *Willamette Writer* for three years. She also served as president and as a board member of the Willamette Writers Association.

Stirling is the mother of five and, when she's not spending time with her kids, works on remodeling her home and pursuing her great love of gardening.

As a frequent explorer of the Oregon Coast, she knows first-hand of its beauty. She says the coast has always been one of her 'get away from it all' places, a place that makes her feel vividly alive.

A native Oregonian, Stirling has lived here a significant part of her life. "I can't imagine what it would be like to never experience this state. There is something about what I call its 'beauty-energy' that touches you in the deepest way."

About the Photographer

The quiet dignity of Larry Geddis is a pleasant surprise in this day of super egos. And he goes about his chosen vocation – photography – in the same quiet, business-like way. But don't let the soft demeanor fool you, for here is a determined, athletic, energetic, and dedicated person who pursues his trade with a passion and an artistic eye, second to none.

Geddis left his school teaching job in 1989 to follow his successful career in scenic photography. And successful he is, with his photos appearing in numerous books, including Beautiful America's *Oregon Coast*, many calendars such as Beautiful America's *Oregon*, *Columbia Gorge* and *Oregon Coast*, along with note cards, magazines and other publications including those of the Portland Chamber of Commerce, Portland/Oregon Visitors Association and the Oregon Tourism Division.

Geddis is an avid backpacker and has hiked repeatedly through the designated wilderness areas of Oregon, always searching for yet another beautiful landscape to photograph.

Sunset on the south coast

*Rear Cover: Colorful kites and banners signal the
annual Lewis and Clark Kite Festival at Seaside*